GOOD GRIEF

Healing Through Reflections

Melvin Collins

RELENTLESS
PUBLISHING

Good Grief : Healing Through Reflections

Printed in the United States of America.

Published by :
Relentless Publishing House
www.relentlesspublishing.com

RELENTLESS
PUBLISHING

ISBN - Paperback : 978-1-948829-65-6

Dedication

In loving memory of my parents, Emma Mae Harvey-Collins and Frank Collins, Sr., who died on March 15, 2015, and October 17, 2018, respectively.

"Death, the only immortal who treats us all alike, whose pity and whose peace and whose refuge are for all – the soiled and the pure, the rich and poor, the loved and the unloved."

Mark Twain

Acknowledgments

Written to those who are grieving because your loved one is no longer present in this world!

TABLE OF CONTENTS

PREFACE

Good Grief: Healing through Reflection is an informative grief journal about the nuances of grief, healthy coping skills, and an anthology of poems. Each poem is an emotional reflection of my grief responses. My hope is that my story can help you process your grief.

The *My Grief Journal* section is an open invitation for you to share your thoughts. I recommend that you use these pages to process your feelings. Don't focus on how your words sound, but rather focus on releasing.

Recovering from the darkness of grief and trauma is universal. While many are battling against the raging tides of life, my hope is that through this grieving process, you will learn how to look beyond the horizon.

Navigating, understanding, and recognizing your grief is your challenge. The expectation of hope, peace, and learning how to smile again is your recovery path. Better days are possible!

WHAT IS GRIEF

Grief is the emotional response to the loss of someone or something of value, to which an attachment was developed. It is often characterized by internal emotional pains that impact ones cognitive, spiritual, and cultural mentality, including feelings of sadness, helplessness, and loneliness. In addition to the internal emotional components, other external symptoms exist effecting the physical, behavioral, and social mentality, including fatigue, social distancing, and lack of focus. The philosophical mentality of grief is universal. During the grieving process one may struggle to adjust to the traumatizing event of physically being absence from their loss. Morrie Schwartz wrote in his book *Tuesdays with Morrie* that "death ends a life, not a relationship. All the love you created is still there. All the memories are still there. You live on in the hearts of everyone you have touched and nurtured while you are here."

The emotional attachments of grief elicit complex feelings during and after a loss. Feelings of psychological and spiritual detachment provoke natural responses. Those responses may cause stress and mental and physical anguish. However, the specific emotions associated with grief are like a constellation of various thoughts and feelings. Those feelings may express themselves at any moment. The exhibited emotional grief responses may be crying, having periods of depression, becoming withdrawn, anger, rage, confusion, and deep sorrow. Physical grief responses may be panic attacks, fast breathing, body aches (stomach/headaches), loss of appetite, loss of sleep, and loss of motivation.

Grief encompasses comprehensive individual experiences. Grief is an inevitable part of every person's life, regardless of gender. Grief is one of the greatest isolating forces. Those who are grieving all too often feel invisible, misunderstood, and unwanted, leaving them grieving in isolation. The "individual experiences of grief vary and are influenced by the nature of the loss" (mayoclinic.org/patient-visitor-guide/support-groups/what-is-grief). The nexus of the relationship, which is the connection or series of connections linking two or more things, persons, or events, is a part of a chain of causation that influences one's grief response.

One of the best examples of a grief response is when one's body is in tremendous pain, but not knowing the causation of the pain. Once the pain overrides comfortability, a decision to seek medical attention is determined. One walks into the doctor's office receiving paperwork. Once completed, the patient is in an examination room. While in the examination room, one of the first questions asked is, "On a scale from 1-10, what is your pain level?" Based upon the amount of discomfort and the severity of the pain, they give a number. However, I have discovered that being able to quantify and identify the pains of the heart is different. The grief response to the pains of the heart cannot be computed on a 1–10 scale. The death of "someone or some living thing" is a traumatic tragedy. The absence of the nexus is an emotional rollercoaster. The grief pain is a constant reminder of the empty void.

The processing of grief is a lifelong journey. The grieving process cannot be minimized. Each person grieves differently. The recovery process does not occur overnight. The death of a loved one changes lives and the dynamics of the family unit forever. The struggle of learning how to deal with the "new normal" prohibits the freedom to identify and express one's traumas of grief.

The bereavement period is the time whereby one mourns their loss by expressing exhibited behaviors such as crying, having periods of depression, and becoming withdrawn. The duration of the bereavement period depends on the nature of the loss, how attached one is to the loss, or the amount of time spent anticipating the loss. Mourning is the act of grieving outwardly. The exhibited behaviors may be the wearing of black clothing, a black head covering, or a black arm band. The response to bereavement and mourning periods is dependent upon one's customs and culture. However, the pathway to recovery is the same.

There are numerous types of grief. I will highlight six. (1) Normal Grief, also known as Uncomplicated Grief, describes the normal emotions associated with losing a loved one. Each person has a normal period of grieving. The grief response of crying is an exhibited behavior while processing their "new normal." (2) Complicated Grief, which describes a grief that worsens over time. The grief deepens and stagnation develops. The person is anxious about their losses and the grief disrupts their daily life. They feel the gravity of their loss all the time, causing them to lose focus on self-care, self-motivation, and self-identity. (3) Compound Grief, also known as Cumulative Grief, is the piling-on effect where many loved ones are lost over a shortened period while experiencing new losses. The same emotions associated with losing a loved one are expressed when those losses may come from different areas of life. Those losses may consist of a relationship, a pet, material items, self-functioning, self-mobility, self-identity, hopes and dreams, and the loss of opportunities. Put together, these losses become a big pile-up of overwhelming grief. (4) Traumatic Grief is grief associated with the traumatic death of a loved one or the distressing experiences of individual traumas resulting from gun violence, domestic violence, or car accidents. Those individual traumas may be sexual, physical, verbal, emotional, or spiritual abuse, divorce, intimidation, or financial hardships. Traumatic grief is triggered by sudden or unexpected events. (5) Delayed Grief is when grief is postponed. The postponed grief often shows up weeks, months, and sometimes years after the traumatic event. The responsibility of trying to be strong during the grieving process often delays the healing process. The delays in grief are triggered by several factors. Grief triggers may be the loss of a parent, child, or other family members, or the experience of additional individual traumas. (6) Anticipatory Grief is when the grief expressed is in advance of a loss. The perceived losses are inevitable. Those losses may come from having a loved one in hospice care due to a terminal illness, a loved one who may be experiencing serious medical conditions, or the anticipated loss of self-functioning. Left untreated, these types of grief can cause physical or mental illness.

Elisabeth Kubler-Ross, in her book *On Death and Dying*, presented the theory about the *Five Stages of Grief*. She suggested that during the grieving process, one experiences five different emotional responses. These responses work in conjunction and fluctuate between each other. The objective is to recognize each stage. These stages are denial, anger, bargaining, depression, and acceptance. An explanation of each is below.

1. **Denial** – is the grief response of defensiveness. It is a mechanism used to buffer the immediate shock of

losing someone or something by numbing the emotional pain. Thoughts and feelings are blocked by fear. Phrases used are "no, this must be a mistake" or "they are coming back."

2. **Anger** – is the grief response of non-verbal communication. It is a mechanism used to mask the emotions of displeasure, annoyance, or hostility. The direction of anger is toward someone you feel has wronged or caused you harm. Anger can be deliberate with levels of resentment toward family, friends, or even the deceased loved one for leaving, doctors for not doing enough, or the part one may or may not have played in their deceased loved one's life. Guilt is often one of the leading contributors associated with anger. Questions asked are "why."
3. **Bargaining** – is the grief response of attempting to secretly make a deal with God or oneself prior to the death of a loved one. Phrases used are "God, if you allow my mother to live, I will …"
4. **Depression** – is the grief response of having an emotional state of sadness or regret causing one to withdraw from society. Phrases used are "I just want to be left alone."
5. **Acceptance** – is the grief response of reaching a state of never getting over losing a loved one, but rather learning how to process the grief. Processing one's grief may include moments of depression and self-doubt; however, there is an acknowledgment that your loved one is no longer present.

Most people operate from the acceptance level fluctuating between these five emotional responses. The emotional fluctuations are raw and instant creating moments of frustration. The phrase "I'm ok" is used to make the true description of feelings. Most people have difficulty finding the correct words to express what their "ok" means. Below are commonly shared emotional responses that can help best identify your feelings.

Abandonment	Aloneness	Anger
Anxiety	Avoidance	Betrayal
Bitterness	Blame	Complaining
Complacent	Confused	Crying
Denial	Dependent	Depressed
Disorganized	Detached	Empty
Envious	Exhausted	Fatigued
Guilty	Heartbroken	Helplessness
Inadequate	Isolation	Jealousy
Lonely	Overwhelmed	Regret
Rejection	Sadness	Sorrow

When I began to identify how I felt abandoned, alone, angry, and heartbroken, things started to change. I compared my grief to a ship lost at sea with no hope and no direction. In the darkness of the night, I had no sharp vision. My poem "Lost at Sea" is my reflection of the surrounding darkness of my grief. My poem "No Goodbyes" is my expression of the heavy price I paid when I lost both my parents. I encourage you not to remain silent in your grief. Do not be afraid to release your feelings. If you are struggling with grief, experiencing thoughts of suicide, having feelings of detachment, sudden changes in behavior, or feelings of depression, please seek treatment from a health care professional. Regardless of how hard life may appear, help is available.

Lost at Sea

Like a ship lost at sea in the darkness of the night
Pitch black, I have no vision trying to understand
Why the waves are crashing
My ship is rocking feeling the motions of the sea
Moving but no land in sight
Oh, I wonder will I ever survive
Searching for calm seashores
My soul cries out, *"Everyone, let's give up.*
Too bleak to go on, there's no hope in sight"
Dropping my shoulders
Placing my head between my knees
Hands are shaking looking for help
But no help is in sight
Then I remembered, there is a captain unseen
"Hold the stern," I heard,
"Straight and tight, rough waves ahead,
But I will guide you through the night"
In the darkness of the night,
I saw a glimmer of light
Not the light of stars nor moon
But the light of my hope
I heard the voice once again,
"You can make it to that peaceful shore"
Quietness exists while waiting
Holding straight and tight
Riding the waves guiding me through the night!

No Goodbyes

Heartache is funny like an albatross tied around my neck
Weights bearing on my chest, pressing through my stomach
The pain and anguish are his leaving cards
He's like a trusted friend
I can count on him to show up anytime, day or night
Going throughout my day functioning as usual
But heartache is right there carrying along the way
Trusted is my friend.
He has never let me down
Trying to send him away, but he's right by my side
He often loves to sit pressing on my chest
We get up in the morning getting ready for the day ahead
Meetings or conference calls, no matter what he is right there
This friend is different, others come and go but he never goes away
Trying to send him away to check on other friends
But he remained right by my side, clearly out of sight
Heartache is that friend that sticks close
Unlike others in the past
Counting on my friend to show up unexpectedly
From the shadows he emerges, I can trust him that way
It never fails, he's always right there
Somedays, I miss heartache
I've gotten used to you being around
Closing another hectic day, laying down to rest,
Heartache is right there having his way
Taking inventory counting the new additions
Made along the way building the platform for tomorrow
Having new playmates for my friend to enjoy
Trying to say goodbye, you really need to go
Only realizing that I'm not saying goodbye
But only saying goodnight!

COPING WITH GRIEF

After losing both my parents, my life took a different direction. The things I considered important and valuable were no longer important. I was trying to figure out how to accept my new normal. I was trying to find answers to questions that seemed unanswerable. So, I made the decision to drop my pride and acknowledge my pain. I had to find the strength to move forward. I started searching for a new path. The only problem was I made the choice to chart a new path, but I did not know how. The present place of my grief was more than what I could manage. The solutions I developed were not the healthiest. I was consoling the symptoms but not analyzing the source. All that changed when I had a conversation with a friend who was experiencing specific medical issues. After countless conversations of asking him how he was doing and getting the same, "I'm doing fine," the day of this conversation things were different. His response was different. When I asked how he was doing, he paused and said, "Not well." He began to talk about the struggles he was facing. He mentioned the appropriate medical terms, some I had heard of and others I had not. I listened while holding the phone while my friend shared his heart. However, the glaring part of the conversation was when he mentioned the things he had lost due to his illness. He talked about his loss of energy, loss of mobility, no longer having a healthy appetite, and not being able to sleep through the night because his body was in pain. As we continued to talk, I quickly discovered the complexities of grief.

I was grieving over physically losing both my parents, but he was grieving over physically losing himself to the mentality of the man he once was. After our conversation, I paused and began to reflect over our shared experiences. We both lost something of value that altered our lives. We both shared our grief moments, reflecting on our past experiences. But his grief was a projection into his future. I thought about those days I could function with thinking about my parents. But his everyday were moments of a view of what his life may evolve into with his body not functioning. Our stories are different but similar at the same time. Two stories of grief are both heartbreaking. For my friend, he started his day by willing his body to function, while I faced mine by willing my heart to face the rising sun.

Over the years, our conversations evolved. Conversations about how we were doing turned into conversations about how we were managing our day. We both discovered we were not processing our grief. We were only functioning. We both were only in motion trying to deal with life. We were not coping with our losses. I was not coping with the loss of my parents. I was deep in an emotional tangle. Nor was my friend coping with losing his bodily functions. When I thought about it, I paused, giving myself time to consider the emotional barriers we built. We both were in a major dysfunction of emotional responses. The more I thought about it, the more I became aware of how I was coping by turning healthy behavior into excessiveness. I found myself overworking, overeating, and overly staying busy by attending church functions. My excessive behavior was my way of trying to console my broken heart by filling time and space. I was coping the best way I knew but I had to learn how to make lemonade from emotional lemons.

Coping refers to the thoughts and behaviors used to manage internal and external stressors. Coping involves adjusting to the unusual demands and negative events of life while trying to maintain a positive emotional equilibrium. The experiences of adjusting to these changes create feelings that the events of life are out of control. Thus, creating stressors that may be cumulative and profoundly making it difficult to maintain physical and emotional healthiness. The coping behavior is either reactive or proactive. Reactive coping is the response that follows a stressor. Stressors like a new purchase, a new marriage, new children, new marital problems, new financial problems, and new losses can influence the behavioral response. These stressors generate an onset of new events. However, proactive coping is an attempt to address long-standing stressors. Stressors like the continued issues in relationships, marital problems, lengthy chronic illness, and the lingering adjustments to the death of a loved one. The stress of losing something of value creates an intense tangled web of emotional responses. The consumption of grief causes one to experience internal pains, external physical exhaustion, and moments of feeling overwhelmed.

The incredulous moments of grief cause an emotional or physical response. These occurrences are emotional triggers, also called mental or psychological triggers. A trigger is a stimulus that elicits a reaction. These triggers may include smells, sounds, songs, a shared memory, certain familiar people or faces, places, special occasions, and familiar situations. The reaction is abrupt and happens within seconds. Faced with emotional triggers, my reaction sparked an intense negative emotion which brought me back to that moment when time stood still. I was devastated. These triggers affected how I felt, how I thought, and how I responded.

A healthy solution was understanding how to cope with stress-related grief. Those who grieve do so by internalizing their thoughts and struggles. I had difficulty outwardly and openly expressing my feelings. People told me to cry in private.

And to keep to privately guarded. However, what they did not know, it created a raging storm. The results are an explosion of sadness, anger, and depression.

I had a conversation with a friend who lost her mother. She shared her heartbreaking story of how she missed her mother. She shared that her mother was older in age and lived a blessed life. But the longevity of her life still did not take away the pain. She talked about her feelings and the things she was going through. I noticed something toward the end of our conversation, she shared a tremendous amount of information in a brief period of time. She was willing to share her painful story. I sat with an attentive ear, hearing the elegant flow of her words as though she was painting an outward canvas. After our conversation, I began to wonder about the similarities and differences between men and women coping and expressing their grief.

The causation and triggers are the same. Both have difficulty sleeping, lose interest in daily activities, and become more irritable as time progresses. However, it does appear that women tend to cope better with grief because they are more willing to share their feelings with friends and family members, and there is a greater willingness to seek emotional support. On the contrary, men are different. They are instructed from childhood a socially different message about expressing their emotions. They are taught "boys don't cry" and to "never show weakness." Meaning, men do not cry. This belief causes men to become sheltered and protective of their hearts and emotions. Men have a natural difficulty talking about their feelings, emotions, and especially their grief. When grieving men defer to logic. Men often make head decisions verses those of the heart. Men compartmentalize their emotions by trying to analyze the specific stressors with a mindset of fixing the problem. Men tend to find it easier to process physical issues while overlooking the emotional ones. Thus, creating internal struggles by remaining silent. Both have the same type of losses, but their responses are different. I responded to my grief out of the abundance of my subjective experiences. My friend who was grieving over losing his bodily functions responded through the lens of his experiences. As well as my friend who lost her mother. All three of us lost something of value, but we all had a different grief response.

As a certified grief counselor, I had to challenge myself to view the practical ways of recovery. Honestly, there are a variety of healthy and unhealthy coping strategies used to manage stressful situations. The choice is not always a binary decision. The choice could simply be, "I don't want to hurt anymore." However, we must be careful not to allow the need not to feel the pain to override conscious, healthy decisions. The key to coping is identifying unhealthy and healthy strategies. Below are common unhealthy masking strategies I have identified individuals use while dealing with their grief.

- Self-medication - overly consuming prescribed painkillers, illegal drugs, or alcohol.
- Self-harm - deliberately injuring oneself by cutting, piercing, punching, or burning to physically feel internal pain.
- Self-isolation - withdrawing from society.
- Procrastination - delaying tasks until the last minute or past their deadline.
- Excessive behavior - taking normal activities and turning them into extreme behaviors:

- o Binge eating or emotional eating, permissive sexual relations, working to the point of exhaustion

Masking the problem is not the solution. I recommend enacting these to help manage those stressors:

- Admit you need help.
- Address your grief with a health care professional.
- Avoid shutting down through the grieving process.
- Ask for personal forgiveness of self and others.
- Apologize to yourself and to others.
- Alter your behavior.
- Accept your new normal.
- Acknowledge your pain.
- Give yourself permission to grieve.
- Understand your grieving process is unique to your experience.
- Understand that grief can trigger different and unexpected emotions.
- Join a support group.
- Focus on positive memories.
- Re-engage in your hobbies and interests.
- Journal your feelings and thoughts.
- Reflect on your spiritual beliefs.

Coping with grief is a process rather than an event. Those who suffer from grief and trauma are more than likely to be susceptible to emotional triggers. Coping with grief elicits certain emotional responses that may require alternating between healthy coping strategies to achieve a positive outcome. The use of unhealthy coping strategies is not an answer. Nor is using mind-altering substances. I have often said the person who drinks excessively as a coping mechanism does not drink because they love drinking, but they drink to silence the raging voices. The alternative is choosing to face the rising sun. Learning how to live life, embracing, and processing grief is critically important. I wrote "Chaos" when my thoughts were raging. The internal pains manifested themselves through feelings of anxiety. My process of dealing with grief started when I began to focus on positive coping skills. I reflected on my spiritual beliefs by leaning into my faith. I acknowledged my pains and admitted I needed help. If you are struggling to cope with grief, please reach out to a health care professional. The storm may rage, but calm seas are possible.

Chaos

Music blasting

Mind racing

Trying to quiet the voices

Overtaking my thoughts

Phone not ringing

I say aloud

"Where are you?"

You're not here

I cry aloud

"Can you help me?"

Silence is my answer

Thinking in my head

Trying to figure

Where to go from here

I softly say in my thoughts

"I don't know, just away from the pain"

MY GRIEF REFLECTIONS

It was the fifteenth of March 2015. A day I will always remember. It was the day that my mama died. I never got the chance to say goodbye. I never got the chance to hear her say my name again. And I never got the chance to hold her warm lovely hands again. Well, it all started on a quiet Sunday morning. I woke up as normal. I walked into the kitchen to fix coffee. I looked out my window. The sun was shining. The birds were chirping. I proceeded to my bedroom. While dressing, my phone rang. As a pastor, a 7:00 a.m. phone call means one or two things: Someone has died, or someone is sick. I answered the phone, and it was my sister. I said "hello," but the call dropped. I tried calling her back, but the only response was her voicemail. I looked out my front window. I noticed that her car was not at her house but at my parents. I quickly put on my shoes not knowing what to expect. I got in my car. I headed to my parents' house. I was nervous but I did not know why. While walking through the front door, I heard my sister screaming. Then I saw her crying, breaking into a million pieces. I saw my father sitting in his chair looking despondent. I asked what was wrong. They did not say a word but could only point toward the kitchen. I mustered up the strength while walking through the kitchen and headed to my mother's room. There in her room, I saw the one thing I thought I would never see. I saw my beloved mother sitting in her chair. She was leaning over as though she was asleep. I called 911 and then waited for emergency services. While waiting for help, I took her by her hand. It was lukewarm to the touch. I checked for a pulse and signs of her breathing. All seemed quiet as she sat in her chair. The EMTs have now arrived. A hopeless feeling while listening to their news. It was the fifteenth of March. A day I will always remember. That was the day my mama died. That was the day my life changed forever.

My memory from that point is hazy. I remember preparing for my mother's funeral. Family and friends were calling and coming by with well wishes. There was so much to do! It felt like time was running out. Deadlines from the funeral home and the program printer were all stressful. We had to prepare for the service. Each of us wrote our own personal tributes. I remember my sister asking me to deliver her eulogy. Oh, what an honor to have the final words said in the presence of family and friends. My dad asked me to sing an old familiar song, *"I Don't Know Why I Have To Cry Sometimes"* by Katie Sankey.

The day of her funeral it was raining outside. How befitting for what I was feeling inside. The local church was only minutes away. But the drive seemed like an eternity. When we arrived at the church. A trusted friend who walked me inside. While standing at the entrance of the sanctuary, I noticed that the church was full. I walked my father, side by side, down that long center aisle where my mother was laying. I was hurting inside but I had no time to grieve. The service was starting. I was present in my body, but my mind was in a different place. I heard the choir singing while they were watching my every move. The time is now approaching for me to deliver the eulogy. I took a deep breath. I steadied my legs. I walked to the pulpit preparing to say my final words. There I was standing on the platform preparing to say goodbye. I sang my dad's favorite song, then turned my mind to say my words. I cannot remember the title of my message, but it was a message about a good soldier living a well-pleasing life and receiving her reward. The moments of her funeral did not feel real, but I had a duty to perform. Looking back, that entire experience reminded me of a song by Freya Ridings, "Lost Without You." Her words inspired me to author my poem "Lost."

However, at the end of the service, I was exhausted. It was the climax to the hardest point in my life. Now that the funeral was over. I told my family and friends thank you as they dined over a grateful meal. When I arrived back home, I told myself it was over. But in reality, it had only begun. I processed through the service but not through my feelings. I continued with life as though nothing had occurred. I treated each day as normal. I told myself, my faith will get me through. My mother's death was unexpected. But as the years passed by, my father became ill. Congestive heart failure was his diagnosis. As time progressed, my father's sickness became worse. After an intense conversation with his doctor, my dad was recommended for hospice care. Hospice care was not about getting better but making his transition more comfortable. It was one of the hardest decisions we had to make. Once in the program, it was a big adjustment. For eight months, he lived in my home living out his remaining days. There was no possibility of recovery and no turning back.

This tall, slender-built man is struggling with his mobility. Looking back, I saw him grieving over the loss of a life he once lived. The things he previously did, he was no longer able to perform. He tried to walk but the feebleness of his body would not allow. I recall my father saying to me, "once a man, twice a child." I understood what he meant. I would tell him "don't worry everything was going to be alright." I would have to lift him from the bed to his chair and take care of all his personal needs. He was embarrassed at first, but there were no other options. He was a proud man but not too proud to receive help. The fact that he would never walk again began to ring large. He would often talk about the things he did in his past. I would sit and listen with an attentive ear. But deep down I know how he wished he could still walk. He never said it aloud. But I saw it in his frustration every time he tried. A constant man of faith believing God would make away. Eventually, he found his inter peace in the silence of the man he used to be.

If you knew my father, you could only love and respect him. He was born during the era of segregation, racism, and sharecropping. He grew up facing discrimination and oppression. I would listen to his stories about how their family struggled to make ends meet. There was an agony in his voice using unspoken words when he spoke about racism and not being afforded the opportunity to complete school nor receive decent employment. Although my mother finished college and was employed as an elementary school teacher, my father was only afforded the opportunity to finish the fifth grade. His schooling was in the sharecropping fields picking cotton, raising livestock, and gardening. He was a man of many skills. God blessed him with the ability to learn. He taught himself how to read and write. He started working as a diesel mechanic and later retired as a shop supervisor. He would often say, "Melvin, the Lord has been good to me. Make sure you work hard, get a good education, and get a good job." While listening to his stories, he lamented about the societal culture of denying people of color from fully being a part of this American experience. Our conversations would often cause me to ponder.

Although my father did not use the word racism, there was a transferable trauma. The compound nature of my grief was triggered by my own personal experiences as well. The delayed effects of my trauma began to surface rapidly as the events of life occurred. The news and social media platforms were showing disturbing images and events that I thought were over. My emotions were unsteady. My father would often tell me not to watch all that, but the draw was greater than I expected. Dr. Martin Luther King Jr. said, "One hundred years later (after the Emancipation Proclamation), the Negro still is not free. One hundred years later, the life of the Negro is still sadly crippled by the manacles of segregation and the chains of discrimination. One hundred years later, the Negro lives on a lonely island of poverty in the midst of a vast ocean of material prosperity. One hundred years later, the Negro is still languished in the corners of American society and finds himself an exile in his own land. And so, we've come here today to dramatize a shameful condition." And furthermore, "America has given the Negro people a bad check, a check which has come back marked 'insufficient funds." As a result of my emotional instability and the triggering of my grief, I wrote the following poems, "Frustration," "Unsteady," "George Floyd," "Colors," "Traumatized," and "Crossroad."

Nevertheless, after my father retired, he never stopped working. Every day there was always something to do. I would often say, "He stays busier now that he's retired than he did when was working." He was a strong functioning man, but time brought about a change. The slow agony of death crept in every day. Our conversations became shorter. I saw his body weathering away. A slow death I saw in a man I knew to be strong and mighty. I took care of my dad as a responsibility. Things of the past no longer mattered. I started cherishing each day. As hard as it was, I had a charge to keep. The last week of his life was the hardest. I would check him each morning to see if he remained alive. I did not know how traumatizing that was until years later. I would hear him praying for God to take his pain away. A desire he had was to go home and to be with the Lord. We were in conflict. I wanted his pain to end but to end with a miraculous healing. God answered us both. In the quietness of the morning, he found his peace. It was the seventeenth of October 2018. A day I will always remember. It was the day that my daddy died. I am grateful for the lessons he taught. But truly, I am grateful I got the chance to say goodbye. I got the chance to hear his voice. I got the chance to hold his warm, lovely hands.

My mother's death changed my life. But my father's death triggered my life. Triggered by emotions hidden inside. I started having reoccurring dreams of what I considered suppressed memories. I did not realize all the baggage I was carrying. Until one day those emotions came flooding like a massive downpour. I was asking myself, "Why am I crying?" Because I did not understand. I was walking on eggshells. Every little thing was making me angry. I had a good friend who saw my behavior. They told me I was grieving the death of both my parents. The traumatizing experience had taken its toll. I chuckled with a laugh and said, "That is impossible." I told my friend, "I have faith in God and my parents are at rest in heaven." My friend said to me "all can be true. They may be in heaven, but they are not here with you." That conversation, as painful as it was, changed my life by giving me a reason to think. For the very first time, I began to grieve the loss of both my parents. I did not understand the emotional price I paid. But I knew the present place of sorrow was a place I could not stay. My dreams of a better tomorrow began to fade away. I was raw with emotions all bubbling inside. I felt the tension of stress piercing through my shoulders. And in that moment, I realized I needed help. I contacted a grief counselor. And I started the long difficult journey of processing my grief. Triggered by so many emotions, I searched for answers, reaching for that impossible cure. I finally came to realize that I was missing both my parents. Overdue was the grief of my mother.

The ignition of my grief was my father. The grief I felt for him was like a mighty stone that weighed me down. I realized that grief was more than losing someone you love. While my father was dying, I was grieving with him over the things he sacrificed and lost. I could only imagine not being able to walk is a scary feeling. Becoming reliant on someone else to meet your basic needs is overwhelming. The looks of uncertainty, wondering what others are thinking, are they helping because you asked or is it something they really want to do. People can be funny when offering what others need. I was able to cope sitting by the bedside of my dying father, offering what he needed when his life took a different turn.

Years later, I recall having a conversation with a pastor. He asked me how I was doing, and I replied as normal, "All is well." After general pleasantries, we began sharing what was new. I told him I was writing about grief and had questions. At first, I did not want to talk but he was curious. I answered his questions while talking about how I missed my mother. I told him writing was my healing process. However, his response blew me away. He proceeded to tell me I should not be grieving my mother because if she was a woman of faith, she was with God. And my grieving was my lack of faith. Initially, his words hurt but I quickly moved to anger. I could not find the words to convey what I was feeling. As I listened to him go on and on, giving me his interpretation about how I should not be grieving for my mother. I gathered my thoughts and said, "Me missing my mother has absolutely nothing to do with my faith in God."

The more I tried to explain the angrier I got. He only heard what he wanted to hear. I quickly ended the conversation by walking away feeling hurt, devalued, and misunderstood. I started questioning my faith, wondering was I wrong for missing her. My questions turned from sadness and sadness to anger. I could not believe how someone who professed to know God would question my faith because I expressed missing my mother. As I sat in the silence of my thoughts, I thought of a song by Meriam Bellina, "*One Day at a Time*." After that conversation, I reminded myself I was taking each day one day at a time. I came to realize that every person is different. And in my humanity, my heart was breaking because I lost my mother. But in my faith, I hold to God's unchanging hands. I vowed that day to never minimize someone else's grief because I may have a different philosophical understanding. Regardless of your level of faith or religious understanding, every person experiences grief.

Dr. Lisa M. Shulman with the American Brain Foundation, said, "Grief is a normal protective process. This process is an evolutionary adaptation to promote survival in the face of emotional trauma." Through therapeutic services, I realized I needed to survive my grief. I had to learn how to express my thoughts and feelings while balancing every day. And I had to learn that the initiation of my grief was not the death of my father, but my mother's death. I did not understand why she had to die. Lost in my thoughts and angry at life, I was depressed because I missed her. I was frustrated because there was nothing, absolutely nothing I could do to bring her back.

I wrote a tribute to her titled "Dear Mama" as my expression of grief. The experience of losing her was difficult. Her legacy lives today in my memories. Today, I am no longer a survivor. I needed more than just existing. I am recovering, recovering from each loss that I have suffered. In therapy, I learned the steps of grief and how to regain a healthy state of mind. I started journaling how I processed my day, my thoughts, and my feelings. I began to write from a difficult place. My poems "Expectations Birth Disappointments" and "Overloaded" are the ramblings of my mind. A therapeutic methodology to my raging thoughts.

<u>Lost</u>

Standing on the platform preparing to say goodbye
Watching you go as they lower the casket door
Taking my last look struggling to say goodbye
The pain of losing you is like no other pain known
I'm feeling out of control crushed from within
Never gave thought to how life would be
Hearing people say, *"Be strong, she's in a better place"*
Yes, I know God makes no mistakes
But in this moment, I'm feeling lost without you
Trying to find my strength while navigating through the pain
You've been my safety and now you're gone to an unreachable place
Standing on the platform preparing to say goodbye
Talking about a good solider gone home to glory
To meet her awaiting Master on the peaceful shores of time
But deep inside, my world is crashing all around
Today isn't normal, all things seem unreal
Trying to press forward but it's taking more than what I can give
Standing on this platform preparing to say goodbye
Giving my all, trying to memorialize your legacy
Being in this space isn't my choice
Inwardly, searching for relief
A place of quietness in my darkest hour
Outwardly, composed
Preaching as though it's another day
Fulfilling my obligations
Telling the entire world about a mother
Who meant the world to me
A Christian solider to the world but to me a beloved mother
Who raised a son embedding the strength
To stand on this platform to say goodbye

Dear Mama

As the years pass by
Missing you increasingly more each day
The sound of your voice
The way you called my name
How you showed your love
In a very caring way
Ointment on my knee
When I fell off my bike
Sitting by my bedside
When I was sick and could not even sleep
Your determined words
To be your best, still sound in my ears
The smile on your face
As I walked across the stage
How you raised my children
With your loving care
They all have a piece of you
In their own distinct way
Our Bible Study lessons
Followed by an afternoon treat
Vanilla ice cream in a cup
A chocolate fudge sundae
When I look in the mirror
Seeing your image in me
The man I am today
Is all because of you
You helped me grow finding my way
I can never repay
The things you did for me
But I can say
Thank you, Mama
For showing me the way
Missing you
Loving you dearly!

Expectations Birth Disappointments

Expectations of various roles and positions held make it hard to grieve. The perception that pastors don't grieve, we rely on our faith trusting God through the pain. The pain never goes away.

The harsh reality is Pastors suffer in silence refusing to express thoughts and feelings in fear of judgment from the very ones they are meant to help. How can you help someone else through their trauma if you haven't dealt with your own?

The truth of the matter is that grief is a daily process of reconciliation with my fears. Fears of letting others down, not holding to that preconceived image of men do not cry, and disappointing God.

People need to understand, pastors are human too.

Instead of looking at the assignment, look at the person.

I have the right to express my grief, sit in my feelings, and figure things out. To take the same advice I've given others.

I no longer ask for permission to grieve, waiting on judgmental responses. I deal with my trauma. It's my choice to determine the man I choose to be.

Expectations of trying to be what others expect is my birth of disappointments!

Overloaded

There was a man who lived on a farm. He had cows, horses, chickens, and one mule. Every morning, he would saddle up his mule heading out for the plowing of the day. He loved that mule. He was a good and diligent worker. Every morning, they would work the fields. From the man's perspective, the mule carried the load by responding to his needs. He could plow long days, rough patches through rain, sleet, and even the heat of the day. Oh, how that farmer loved that mule. The more he loved him, the more he worked him. The more he worked the mule, the more the mule grew tired, and the work became too much. One day, the mule began to slow down under the pressure of the load. The same rough patches he worked on were now overwhelming. During the plow, the mule broke down to his knees under the pressure of the load. The farmer began to unbuckle, relieving him from the pressures of the plow. They both stood in the middle of an unfinished row.

The farmer stared at the work, thinking the mule only needed a momentary break. He quickly discovered that was not the case. While the mule stood broken in the middle of an unfinished work, down on his knees, he stayed trying to catch his breath, inhaling and exhaling with the sun beaming down on his back. As the mule regained his breath, his strength slowly returned. The farmer was pleased as he walked his mule back to the barn. The next morning, the farmer gets up, preparing for the same day's work. He puts on his overhauls, boots, and cap, making his way down to the barn. But today is different. The mule is in a different place. The farmer tries to place the yokes of the plow around his neck. The mule constantly moves away, avoiding the straps of the day. The farmer is lost in confusion, wondering why his mule didn't want to work the plow today. As the day grows long, the farmer and mule found themselves in a dance. The farmer trying to buckle his mule, while the mule is avoiding the buckling.

Frustration

Struggling to find the words to express how I feel
Events of the past few years, continued conversations about
The advancement of our people, fighting for equality is like a mental chain
Trying to remain hopeful while playing Sam Cooke in the background
Dreaming of the day when a change will come
Trying to hold my peace and not respond out of frustration
Seeing posts sharing thoughts and prayers
Expressing words of love quoting from the Bible
Hmm, shame! Speaking God but where are your Godliness
Insulting to my intelligence, my biblical theology
Hearing your words, followed by ungodly actions
Your words of change ring hollow
Seeing your actions raises questions
About how you can say you love God
Who you have never seen but hate people who look like me
There's a hatred from within, rotten to the core
It's time to stand up and fight for that promised freedom
The freedom of Heaven in my future goal
But today I fight to be free here on earth
Fighting against the flawed language of a suppressive theology
Leaving millions frustrated
Trying to figure out how to manage this current societal structure
My frustrations, covered with a silent voice
Choosing to no longer sit in this silent place
Cause my frustrations are like a baby's stain
Remaining in the crib while sleeping on dirty sheets
Deciding to have influence, choosing to get up

My mother would often say,
"Bitter and sweet can't come out the same tap"
Time for the mirror to no longer remain silent

James H. Cone wrote
A Black Theology of Liberation
"The function of theology is that of analyzing the meaning of that liberation for the oppressed so they can know that their struggle for political, social, and economic justice is consistent with the gospel of Jesus Christ.
Any message that is not related to the liberation of the poor in a society is not Christ's message.
Any theology that is indifferent to the theme of liberation is not Christian theology.
In a society where persons are oppressed because they are Black, Christian theology must become black theology.
A theology that is unreservedly identified with the goals of the oppressed and seeks to interpret the divine character of their struggle for liberation"

Unsteady

Raging in the darkness wishing someone could hear
Angrily consumed with a fire of hopelessness
Wishing things were different but no differences in sight
Where is my voice, that whisper unheard
I'm angry at the silence, the intolerance, and the injustice
Often hearing people say, *"Justice is Blind"*
Yes, she's blind to race, status, and creed
It doesn't matter who you are
Everyone should get a fair shot, make, or miss
2020 has proven true, *"Justice is Blind"*
She's blind to justice, blind to violence,
Blind to the voiceless, blind to the poor,
Blind to the immigrant, and blind to the helpless
It's true no justice, no peace
Internal rest eludes me
I'm angry, consumed with helplessness
Gun violence is on the rise, people dying
Children starving and I cannot be effective
One plate, two plates, or three
There's so much undone
I hear the cries of your pain
The brokenness of your heart
The torment of your families
The effects of your empty chairs
Reality is harsh, there're no more hugs,
No more kisses, not even a warm goodbye
In these moments of darkness, I rage anger
Trying to hold to the Word where it says,
"Be still and know that I am God"
You're gone too soon, but never forgotten!

In memory of Breonna Taylor and Tamir Rice

George Floyd

Laying alone on the ground pleading for help
People are watching as I suffer crying alone
I hear voices yelling stop no one is coming to my rescue
My energy is fading
Bodies standing while hands frozen
Eyes watch this injustice
I can't catch my breath
The pressure is too much
Wondering what I have done
Making cruelty today's prescription
I can't breathe, I say it repeatedly
I'm afraid, I feel so alone, while eyes are watching
My life is slipping away
I am so afraid I won't make this round
Mama, can you help me
Mama, please help your baby boy
Who is this in the distance a figure unknown
I hear voices talking, singing in the background
On the wings of the morning dove
I can now fly away
He is taking me away from here
As the eyes of those who stood by
Watching my lifeless body weeping and mourning
Crying, another life gone too soon
What will be different, America
How do we fix a broken system
Are we just going to continue looking and pretending

Saying aloud, nothing to see here, all is well
Yes, George Floyd, we failed you please forgive our inaction
I'm praying tonight for justice to right this wrong
As America stands in judgment
This broken system, justifying injurious behavior
What will be different
Are we remaining the same
The same solution remains
Only looking and pretending, seeing nothing
Yes, we all failed you, George
I failed you, George please, forgive my inaction
As we wait for justice that reaches beyond the grave!

Colors

What is it about my complexion that scares you the most
Is it the smoothness of my skin, the imperfections of my freckles,
The firmness of my structure, or the darkness of my tone
Is it my intelligence, my ambitious drive, or my charismatic
presentation
That illuminates behind the beauty of my complexion
Are we going backward, recreating judgment by skin color
What really invites us to sit at the banquet table
Are you more comfortable with reflections of you
Do you only see a system worker fitted for behind the scenes
Should we be unseen, unnoticed but whose work stands undeniable
What is it that scares you the most
You are the steward standing at the crossroad of decisions
The access to the executive room, the job interviewer, the resume
stiffer
What is it that scares you the most
Is it my name, my race, the complexion of my skin, or my talents
Tipping the blind yet peaking scales of equality!

Traumatized

The news is on showing videos looping
Facebook is sharing
Twitter is trending…
One, two, three, four
Black men dead in the street
Five, six, seven, eight
Black men pulled over while driving black
Nine, ten, eleven, twelve
Black men incarcerated
The weight of injustice is overwhelming
When will it stop
When will Black men become more valuable than animals
The perception of others is the news of today
Just another story leading into commercial break
Justice, stop being blind
It's time to take notice of what everyone sees

Crossroad

Two groups, one screaming and the other silent
Standing at the crossroad in this American experience
Seeing the same injustice
But walking away with different perspectives
A bittersweet cup sautéed with self-preservation
One is wrestling not to see while the other has eyes shut
Silence, shouldn't be our option
Dr. King's letter from the Birmingham jail spoke the truth
It's not the one who screams in the crowd that causes fear
But the one who's silent seeing injustice, but for self-preservation
They look the other way
The price of keeping a status overrides justice
The silence of the crowd has caused this American experience
To become a dream!

"In the end
We will not remember the words of our enemies
But the silence of our friends."
Dr. Martin Luther King Jr.

Poetic Reflections

Sunday Morning

Sunday morning, the highlight of my week
Sunday School and Church all starting with Sunday morning breakfast
Waking up with anticipation, the sun shining through my window
Sounds in the kitchen followed by a sweet aroma
Pots and pans ringing while singing a favorite tune
It's my mother doing her Sunday morning thang
She's cooking breakfast and dinner, all at the same time

Breakfast menu:
Homemade biscuits, fried chopped steak, bacon, eggs,
Grits, and my favorite…homemade sugar syrup
Wow, what a lady cooking such a meal
Running to wash while throwing on clothes
My seat awaiting as my father prepares to say grace
I can hear him say, "God, we thank you for our daily bread"
Man, what a meal, I'm full as a tick!
While mama eating too, but still cooking on the stove

Dinner menu:
Fried chicken, mustard greens, mac & cheese,
Homemade peach cobbler
If I could, I'd eat dinner right now!
How did she manage all of this on Sunday morning?
While I'm playing around, the kitchen already clean
Dinner awaiting and Mama's dressed for Sunday School

What an amazing lady! Not for her cooking skills
But for her loving care, time management, and administration
You see, I learned from my mother how to multi-task
Take advantage of time and properly administrate my day
Mama is gone now; Sunday mornings aren't the same
Sweet memories of a lady I called
My mama!

The Empty Chair

Two chairs in a room both facing center stage
Sitting down in one but the other one is empty
Finding myself talking aloud
Reminiscing about the memories we shared
No one is listening but there's a presence in the room
In the space of the empty chair, I say out of frustration,
"Who's there?"
But silence is the reply while staring into space
Seeing the empty chair, I want to kick it over
Fighting through my pain, anger emerges
Struggling from the silence
The empty chair consumes my space
Oh, I yearn for somebody to sit
So, I can stop looking
At the empty chair before me!

Alone

Thought I was alone with no escape
Secretly wishing standing by the seashore
Needing a presence in my space
Crying aloud, *"Is anybody here?*
"Are you listening? Can you stop the pain?"
Watching from a distance, I needed your help
Wanting to be alone; but alone is not good for me
Standing by the sea searching for peace
The pain is overwhelming, it is too much for me
Wanting to shrink away and watch the days go by
Wishing wish it would rain, that's perfect for me
Hoping in the silence
The drops would hide the tears of my pain
Calling your name, but you're not here
You're face dances through my thoughts
Remembering our times
Wanting to be alone
But honestly, not really
Talking through my thoughts
Wondering about the future
Missing your presence
Feeling alone!

The Wave

The wave of joy, it never came
Empty days overwhelmed with despair
Expectations of hope giving only ineptitude
Tears anticipated, hmm one or two drops appeared
The wave should've happened explosion on the way
Disappointment awaiting overshadowing the horizon
Impatient, pain, and confusion are the tides of today
Wishing each wave would take away

Sitting

Sitting alone in my room all dolled up
Phone in hand, keys on my side
Visions of hanging out
Full of laughter and fun
All dressed up with nowhere to go
Sitting alone in my room
Wanting to be happy
Overwhelmed with self-doubt
Thoughts of what I should've done
Wondering who's calling
What would I say
Crying, in the silence of my thoughts
Hearing a faint voice,
"Remain strong, I'm always with you"
My heart is heavy
Believing these words are true
Sitting alone desiring a place just for me

Unchanged

Please, don't change what you see
What you see is all I have
May not be much, but it's all of me
My mind, a worn-out carpet
Where I pace comfortably
Tattered curtains and broken blinds
Are my protection
My desires are simple
Only looking out
Don't see me
Sorry about the furniture It's only one chair
I wasn't planning on sharing
Please, don't change what you see
What you see is the way for me!

Tell Me What You See

What do you see when you look at me
My occupation, all the things I do
The rhythmic flow of my heart
Full of pains, struggles, and fears
The man behind the mask
The guy standing holding broken pieces
The patient without a doctor
Sick without a label
Struggling with a problem
No solution
Let me tell you what I see
A fatherless child
Missing his father while broken by life
Desiring to hear a familiar voice
An early morning song of a favorite hymn
Trying to find comfort in a distant memory
Wishing I can hear my father sing

"The world from you withholds of its silver and its gold
And you have to get along with meager fare
Just remember, in his word, how he feeds the little bird
Take your burden to the Lord, and leave it there
Just take your burden to the Lord oh and leave it there
If you trust him through your doubt, he will surely bring you out
Take your burden to the Lord, and leave it there
If your body suffers pain and your health you can't regain
And your soul is slowly sinking in despair
Jesus knows the pain you feel, he can save and he can heal
Take your burden to the Lord and leave it there!"

Unexpected

Gloomy days, they come and go
Fading into the distance of emotional rage
Time was my only solution
Inwardly retreating now looms
Inclining to emerge what's unknown
Considering my faithful charge
Searching for His presence in my Sanctuary
Re-emerging to embrace a connection once loss
Peace beyond understanding
The sweet presence of God!

Life Impossible

Living life without hurt is impossible
Loving without hurt is impractical
Naively believing the ones I love
Asking myself,
"Do I offer more than what I receive?"
Life's not fair
Fairness, not a part of life
Choosing to give
Choosing to be compassionate
Choosing to be naïve
Choosing to see the good
Are life's prescriptions
When the possibility of hurt is present
True happiness, not coming from people
But in faithful possibilities
Learning is discovery
Giving is the plan
Expecting no return is wisdom
Survival is what's known
Jumping is the plan
Falling is the expectation
Happiness is what's desired
Disappointment returned
Changing perspectives is the result
Crying is my option
But living is the plan!

Friend

Looking through the glass of time seeing cuts, bruises, and scars
Hearing laughter in the distance, invitations sent
Received was the reply expecting my friend to stand by my side
No longer inviting my friend to join this lonely space
'Cause joining never ended well
Friend, you're pleading to come and sit
Here we go again, another invitation sent
Inviting you to join this disastrous space
True to form, invitation accepted
Unsurprisingly, friend, you didn't stay long
The room looked good, from the outside
Once inside, you started noticing the tattered curtains
Holes in the wall, cracks in the floor
Hearing you say, *"You wanted to come inside"*
Only to wonder if I should've kept the door closed
You didn't say a word, but your actions spoke loudly
Seeing it in your eyes, your body language tells the story
Wanting to exit stage right
You hoped I wouldn't notice, the squirming and trembling
My friend speaks, but not to seek, not knowing what to say
You asked the question, *"How are you?"*
Not giving time to answer, as you move into talking about your day
It seems to me, my problems are too much for you
My friend found time to give me words of encouragement,
"Your mind is confused, your thoughts are wondering, think positive
Everything is going to be okay"
I'm crying now inside for my friend
'Cause what I need, you can't give
Uncomfortable spaces aren't for you
So, I return to my space
Looking through the glass of time!

What I Need Today

What I need today is a friend who knows what to say
When skies are blue, and times are hard
Saying more than, *"It's going to be alright"*
What I need today is a friend who sees me for me
Beyond the value of my skills, offering me the safety
Instead of the criticizing and critiquing
What I need today is a friend full of love and care!

Hello

"Hello"
Hey, how's it going
"Who is this"
How's your night
"I was trying to sleep"
"Who is this and why are you talking to me"
It's for you to discover but I saw you tossing
While counting the paces of your thoughts
"Who is this and why are you counting my thoughts"
I AM the voice in the darkness, the breeze you cannot see
I AM the warmth you feel, the storm in a darkened sky
I AM your comforter, your peace in times of trouble
"Why are you here"
I'm here because you called me, I heard your plea for help
While crying in your sleep, you called me by name
When you cried have mercy, meaning you needed me
"Yes, I need thee, my soul, broken and my mind is restless
Crying is my desperate plea while searching for a place of peace
Do not leave me alone, like other have before
Grant me if you please
A safe space so I can feel the breeze!"

Expectation of Disappointment

The expectation of disappointment is a heavy weight
Disappointing looks from familiar faces
They think I should've had a different response
Simply, because I hold certain titles
I should've moved on with business as usual
Their perception, to them, is right
I should've known how to manage my grief
Relying on my faith, my training, and pressing through my pain
The reality is the pain of grief never goes away
I suffer in silence, often refusing to express
My thoughts and feelings in fear of being judged
People harshly say, how can you help others
When you need help yourself
The truth of the matter is grief is a daily process
Of reconciliation while facing my losses
The fear of letting others down
Holding on to that preconceived image
And the pressure of disappointing God
I'm human too
Instead of looking at my assignment, look at me
I have the right to express my grief
To sit in my feelings, and figure things out
Entitled to take the same advice I've given others
Today, I no longer ask for your permission
Waiting for your judgmental thoughts
It's my choice to grieve in the way that is best for me
I will overcome the low bar of your expectations of
disappointments!

Breaking Dam

I thought it was tight
All put together
The raindrops began to fall
My dam started to break
Trying to quickly make repairs
But the breaking is coming too fast
It's all falling apart
I'm feeling hopeless
Consumed with despair
I need someone to help
Trying to keep it all together
My dam is breaking
With floods of emotions
Overwhelmed by fear
I don't know what to do
I need a place of safety
To steady myself
To stand as I face today
Securely holding for tomorrow
In the darkness of the night
Trying to keep the dam together
To be for others what I need for me
I couldn't stop the break
The dam breaking too fast
The waters are overtaking
Pushing me down an unknown path
I wish someone would help
My dam is opening wide
All I can do is hold steady and tight
As I drift during the night!

Selfish

Why call me selfish when prioritizing me
The things I've done for others are now my reward
Why call my demands untimely cringing in dismay
The presentation of what I need is the agenda of today
Thoughts of you being uncomfortable shrunk me in the past
With every denial rescheduling was the order
Keeping silent and accepting was the old prescription
Remembering, yielding my fate while bearing my heavy tears
Sacrifices made were mostly for others
Placing myself first is no longer a request
Ignore at your own expense but your silence speaks volumes
I should've taken care of me, but it's not too late
I'm not asking much just the expectation of my needs
New menu coming soon
Self-care, self-love, and self-nurturing with a side of self-
encouragement
Topped with self-reflections
Hoping, not repeating the same old mistakes
Calling me selfish is a badge of honor
Choosing to wear it well with every forward step
I've made my decision
The space I placed others, I now place me!

I Can’t Sleep

I can’t sleep, there’re images dancing in my head
Of things I can’t remember
Waking up abruptly, sweating from head to toe
Heart racing, chest tight, head pounding
With every heartbeat
Overwhelmed with anxiety, worried about something
I cannot remember
My memories are escaping me like a racer fleeing the starting line
Waking up reaching for help but no one in sight
The nighttime scares me afraid to fall asleep
The terrors of my dreams seem to revisit me
Wide awake watching the darkness of the night
Waiting for the new day
To replace the images in my head!

Not a Good Day

Today, is not a good day
Should be better
Tried to be strong
But stuck in this space
Thinking of you
And the memories we shared
Tried to be my best
My head is a basket case
Tried to say my prayers
My mind is drifting away
Full of shared memories of yesterday
Today, is not a good day
I'm in my feelings
Miss you dearly
Wishing I had more time
To celebrate you in life
My days are full of memories
Mostly, shared with joy
Today, is not a good day
Tomorrow is on the way
But at least I tried today
To make it a good day!

I Thought…

I thought I was alone walking life's journey
Thought the room was empty while sitting in the chair
Thought I only noticed the brokenness surrounding me
But found safely in your arms
The poem is true about the footprints in the sand
What I could not carry, you carried for me
The steps in the sand are the set of my Savior
My burden barrier
The weight of every loss not fitted for me
Now I know the quiet voice
The voice that echoes in the darkness
It's my comforting peace coming to my rescue
My lifeline of hope coming down from above
Pulling me back from the darkness of the abyss
Eddie Cane said, *"I believe I can go"* in the movie *The Five Heartbeats*
My life has left scars and tender places
My head is treading above water
While walking through the waves
I'm going to be all right
Remembering the things my parents said
The joy of the Lord is my strength
Even when the footprints are one!

My Lifter

The choices I made were yesterday's choices
But today I choose to give my all
I give my all to myself
And to the lifter of my head
I entered His perfect peace
Where I found the relief, I sought
I turn to the One who can lift me up
The Lifter of my head
My shield under the eagle's wings
Your love has lifted me
From the shadows of my past
Your love has lifted me
To be the best of what you see!

<u>**Faded Memories**</u>

Faded memories are like a flood
Rushing back from the darkness of the night
The internal pains are overwhelming
Unwanted hands, unwanted touches
Gripped by fear, pain, and unanswered questions
Trying to reach within to soothe an aching heart
Self-serving barriers are guarding the gates of the break
Drifting on the sea, lost on the planks
The waves are carrying me, destinations unknown
My mind is searching for a resting place
Fighting through the tears
The nervousness of uneasy thoughts
Searching for a welcoming memory
I thought I had forgot
Putting my head down, pressing through my life
Pushing down feelings
Holding back tears while living in silence
Walking in darkness needing and not receiving
Then one day I heard a sweet voice
Conversating with me
A voice concerned about me
Relaxing my shoulders, opening my heart
Darkness turned into light
Light turned into hope
Hope turned into dreams!

Anonymous Author

My Grief Journal

My Grief Journal

I'm grieving the loss of…

My Grief Journal

I'm feeling…

My Grief Journal

I need…

My Grief Journal

I'm coping by…

<u>My Grief Journal</u>

I wish I could…

My Grief Journal

My fondest memories are…

My Grief Journal

Memories are like…

My Grief Journal

I'm overwhelmed by…

My Grief Journal

I'm afraid of…

My Grief Journal

I'm trying to forgive myself for…

My Grief Journal

I'm trying to forgive you for…

<u>My Grief Journal</u>

My feelings are like…

<u>My Grief Journal</u>

I'm having a hard time…

My Grief Journal

Expectations are like…

<u>My Grief Journal</u>

The weight of my grief is like…

My Grief Journal

I'm processing my grief by…

About the Author

Dr. Melvin Collins is the father of four children, Desaree, Corey, Calabe, and Melvin Jr. He's the pastor of St. Matthew M.B. Church in Jackson, MS. He's the chaplain supervisor at the Mississippi State Hospital and the moderator for the Counties of MS Baptist District Association. Dr. Collins received his bachelor of arts in business administration from the University of Southern Mississippi, master of Christian counseling and doctoral of theology from the New Foundation Theological Seminary, master of arts in grief counseling, and a specialist of education in trauma informed crisis intervention counseling from the Wellington Institute. Dr. Collins is the cofounder of Good Grief Counseling Services, LLC, and a partner with Combined Human Services, where they provide counseling services. Through Good Grief Counseling Services, he facilitates various conferences, lectures, and training sessions. Dr. Collins is a certified grief, trauma, and crisis intervention counselor through the American Institute of Health Care Professionals. He has served as the dean of Bachelor Studies for New Foundation Theological Seminary, certified dean of Standard Leadership Training Schools through the Sunday School Publishing Board, which is affiliated with the National Baptist Convention, USA, Inc., and dean of Congress for the Counties of MS Baptist District Association. Dr. Collins is the author of *God's Revelation: A Compelling Image of God's Achievable Future for Humanity* and *The Art of Preaching & Teaching: A Homiletical Guide.* Dr. Collins's passion is to holistically help the suffering community by focusing on a Kingdom Focus Ministry.

Made in the USA
Columbia, SC
30 May 2025

58694834R00059